I0517791

FIVE GALLON BUCKET

JACK FRAZIER

QUILL HAWK PUBLISHING

Copyright © 2024 by Jack Frazier

All rights reserved. No part of this book may be used or reproduced in any manner whatsoever, including the purpose of training artificial intelligence technologies under Article 4(3) of the Digital Single Market Directive 2019/790; Quill Hawk Publishing and the author(s) expressly reserves this work from the text and data mining exception. Only brief quotations embodied in critical articles or reviews may be allowed.

ISBN: 978-1-965142-25-7 (Paperback)

ISBN: 979-8-9900749-3-4 (Hardback)

CONTENTS

1

FIVE GALLON BUCKET

Well, hell, I dreamed about basketball again last night. I'm 88 years old and haven't touched a basketball in over 20 years. I still play golf, but I have never been a good golfer. To explain myself, I started playing basketball in the fourth grade. My dad was an engineer in the oil business and our family was transferred all over Texas. This move brought us to a place just north of Borger, Texas. I was placed in a small country school. The principal led me to my classroom, where the teacher introduced me to the class. I looked around the room and stuck out my chest; I decided I could *whip* every boy in the room.

Recess brought a smile to my face. In the other schools, the teacher gave us a football. But this school was different. Since the weather was colder, the teacher marched us into the gym, lined us up at the free throw line, and said, "If you can make a free throw, then you can shoot until you miss."

The girl in front of me hit two shots in a row. Then my turn. I have seen a ball before, but nothing larger than a softball. I shot the ball with one hand like the others. The ball flew over the backboard, and everyone laughed.

I thought I was the toughest; however, I knew I was the weakest at shooting a basketball. That night, I told my dad that I wanted a basketball for my birthday. On my birthday, as promised, I got a brown rubber basketball. I was so happy now; I would show the class who could shoot a basketball. l went outside and suddenly realized I didn't have a basket.

Out in the garage was an old rusty five-gallon bucket; back then they were made of metal—short and wide. With a chisel and hammer, I quickly cut out the bottom, creating a basket. Looking around, I picked out a tree to use as a goalpost. I didn't know a regulation basketball goal was ten feet high, and I just made my best guess.

Now I had a basketball hoop and a goal. I shot and shot; I was having fun. I remember that my mom would call me to come in and practice my guitar lesson. "No!" I said, "I'm quitting guitar lessons!"

Our little country school was having a box dinner as a fundraiser. The boys would bid on the box dinner and eat with the girl. I asked the prettiest girl in my class to be my girlfriend, and I would buy her a box dinner. She looked like I had hit her in the face. She turned and ran laughing over to her girlfriends; they looked at me and laughed.

At the boxed dinner, the ugliest girl, Henrietta, with freckles on her face, could not sell her boxed dinner. So, without me knowing, my mom felt sorry for her and bought her box dinner for fifty cents. That may not seem like a lot of money, but back then, my allowance was fifteen cents a week, so I ate with Henrietta.

Days later, my dad picked up my basketball to examine it. "What has happened to this basketball? I paid two dollars for this ball, and it has scratches all over it. If you tear it up, you will not get a new ball."

"Dad, it's my goal, and the bottom has sharp edges." I showed my dad the five-gallon bucket, and he said, "I will get you a real goal for Christmas."

"Can I have a net also?" I asked.

"OK, that will be your Christmas present," Dad said.

Everything was great, except I did not have a backboard. So, I nailed my new goal to a telephone pole. The bad thing was the pole was on a hill. So, if I missed, I had to chase the ball down the hill. By the fifth grade, I had become the best basketball shooter in school. I often wondered what happened to that five-gallon bucket that was still nailed to that tree.

After the fifth grade, we were transferred to Andrews, Texas. The highlight of the fifth grade was that the coach allowed me to dress out with the eighth-grade team. The coach put me in the game and told me to call time out, according to those old rules. Someone passed me the ball and I got fouled. My coach was mad.

I couldn't believe I was going to shoot a free throw. After I had spent hours shooting at the five-gallon bucket, I went to the free-throw line for the first time in a real game. I looked at the goal and it looked like a five-gallon bucket. I released the ball with a gooseneck follow-through, and the ball went into the basket. My mom was so happy. My dad smiled. Coach was still mad.

My last thoughts of the fifth grade were: I may not be the toughest, but I was the best at shooting a basketball. When we arrived in Andrews, Texas, my dad made me a wooden backboard and put my goal in the backyard. I got ready for the up-and-coming year.

I found out that Andrews brought a new challenge—football. I really wanted to be a star at playing football. By the ninth grade, I was five feet six inches tall and weighed 115 pounds. The coaches were not impressed. However, basketball was different. I got a uniform in the eighth grade.

Our team was playing Kermit, Texas, and we were down by six points, with a little more than two minutes left in the game. I don't know why, but Coach put me in the game. I really think that he had given up on winning and wanted me to get a little playing time. Something happened to me that I had never told anyone, but I felt I was in a dream.

The baskets turned to five-gallon buckets in the last two minutes. I took four shots and made them all. Our team won at the buzzer. The highlights of this game were in the local newspaper, and from then on, I was a starter.

2

5'11 AND THREE QUARTERS

I was on my way to Hobbs, New Mexico when I noticed that their high school team was playing Borger, Texas. I decided to see the game. I noticed a cheerleader from Borger. She was the most beautiful girl I have ever seen. I moved closer and discovered that she had freckles. My God, it was Henrietta! She was gorgeous, and I was afraid to approach her because I treated her so awfully in grade school. I was ashamed of myself.

As a sophomore in high school, I made the all-district team and repeated as a junior. Our coach, who was my uncle, was fired. He had an outstanding record, but Andrews was a football school and jealousy prevailed. This was my mother's brother, and it made us angry. About this time, my dad was being transferred to Hobbs, New Mexico, so I transferred to Blackwell, Oklahoma. This was the town where my mom and dad grew up, and where I was born.

I made the all-district team in Blackwell and was the leading scorer on the team. Our team was defeated in the state semifinals by Putnam City High School. Our high school coach took us to Oklahoma City University where the great coach, Abe Lemons, offered me a half scholarship. The only other college offer came from Hank Iba of Oklahoma State. He offered me an army cot to sleep on. I looked at my two options and chose Oklahoma City. After one semester, coach Abe Lemons called me into his office.

"Jack," Abe said, "I need to be honest with you. I really admire your skills. If you were three inches taller you would start and maybe be an all-American, but with your size and speed," he shook his head and said, "you have the shooting skills, but you just don't have the body. Sorry."

After my meeting, I decided to transfer to Wichita State with the great coach, Ralph Miller. Coach Miller offered me a half scholarship. At Wichita, Ralph Miller liked to start practice by letting the players play a game of horse. So stupid me, I challenged Joe Stevens, an all-American, to a game of horse. Joe laughed in my face. He said to me, "Before you can challenge me to a game of horse, you have to first beat all the other players on the floor, and then you can challenge me."

A month later, with a smile on my face, I approached Joe Stevens, and he said, "OK."

We started our game of horse. It took four practice sessions to complete one game of horse, but I prevailed. Joe said, "You lucked out! Let's play again!"

"No," I said, "before you can play me you have to beat all the players on the floor! Then we can talk about another game."

I excelled at a defensive drill the coach always had us run. I would be on one side of the lane, a whistle would blow, and I would defensively slide to the other side of the lane, pick up a chalkboard eraser, and then defensively slide back and place the eraser on my starting side of the lane. The coach was impressed; I might not be fast, but I was exceptionally nimble.

After my third semester, Ralph Miller called me in for a conference, and I thought to myself, "Here it goes again."

"Jack, you have all the skills; in fact, your shooting is tops! I love your shooting, but I don't see you getting much playing time. You have the skills but don't have the body to compete at this level. I'm sorry to tell you, but you will be on the bench."

After my talk with Ralph Miller, it brought back an old memory.

I was in the eighth grade and in the Boy Scouts. All the towns in West Texas would send their boys to a ranch in the Davis Mountains during the summer. I had advanced to the finals of the contest. As I approached the archery range, I saw my opponent; he was a giant over six feet tall and 200 pounds. Then I noticed he was eating raw hamburger meat.

"Hello, my name is Wahoo McDaniel, and I am from Midland," the raw-hamburger-meat-eating fellow said.

I reached out to shake his hand, and he somehow knocked me over. I rolled down the hill. The scout master that ran the archery range told him not to do that again. Later, I found out that he became an all-American football player at the University of Oklahoma, then an all-pro linebacker in the NFL for the Houston Oilers. He moved on to the Denver Broncos, New York Jets, and Miami Dolphins. Later in life, he became a professional wrestler with the Worldwide Wrestling Federation (WWF).

I didn't know all that. I thought it was a match between a big body and skill. And I won the match! The only other time that I ran into Wahoo McDaniel was when our eighth-grade basketball team played Midland's eighth-grade team. When we arrived at their gym, Wahoo was standing outside Chagga, lugging a gallon of milk. As we walked into the gym, Wahoo pointed at me and said, "I know that one!" He then walked inside the gym and started shooting shots from half-court. As I recall, he wasn't making anything but was going wild with one hook shot, then a jumper. Their coach just shook his head.

I told my coach that I was getting a sick stomach and didn't think I could play.

"Wrong," my coach said. "In fact, you will be guarding Wahoo." The coach was kidding, and everyone laughed.

Years later, I discovered why the great coach, Ralph Miller from Wichita State, would start practice with a game of horse. No wild shooting!

We had seen Wahoo McDaniel when Midland Junior High played our football team. Wahoo killed us. I wanted to play football, but I'm happy to say I sat on the bench and didn't get into the game. We also played Midland's baseball team. I will always remember getting a hit; I'm right-handed, and the outfield moved left. My hit went over the first baseman's head. I made it to second base. The second baseman called time out and said something to the pitcher. They then called time in, and I took a little lead off second base. The second baseman tagged me out on the hidden ball trick. I got red in the face, and the coach was mad.

I contacted my uncle, who coached me at Andrews. He was my mother's brother and was part Cheyenne. His nickname was Chief. He had played football at Pittsburg State and knew the basketball coach. I wrote a letter to the basketball coach at Pittsburg State, and

Chief gave him a phone call. I was offered a scholarship sight unseen. And yes, I am part Native American and am registered as a Cheyenne. I was born in Blackwell, Oklahoma, and since my mother had attended Indigenous school, she was ordered by law to register her children as Native Americans.

I waited in line outside the great John Lance's office. Finally, I walked in to see this great coach.

"How tall are you?" That was the first thing he asked me.

Well, I thought, here we go again. "I'm six feet," I said.

"Kick off your shoes and step on these scales. You are five feet, eleven and three-quarters."

"But with my shoes on, I am six feet," I said.

The coach was determined and said, "The program will list you at 5'11 and three quarters." Next, Coach asked, "You weigh 150 pounds?"

I responded, "I usually weigh 155 pounds."

"You don't look like Chief! Was your mother the red-headed Indian?" Coach Lance asked.

"Yes, I'm a registered Cheyenne."

I spent three years at Pittsburg State. I was happy to be a starter during my junior and senior years. I was able to complete my B.S. degree in education and later two Master of Science degrees—Physical Education and Guidance Counseling. Now, to start my coaching career.

Each day, I would go to the placement bureau looking for a job. It disappointed me that the only job I was offered was a junior high job in Texas, near El Paso. I coached an undefended football team and my basketball team won about half of their games.

The following year I moved to Hobbs, New Mexico. I was the ninth-grade basketball coach at Highland Junior High School. I didn't know it at the time, but I coached under the great Ralph Tasker. Coach Tasker played college basketball at West Virginia in a small college. He was told by a doctor that his wife would have to move to a dry climate or die young, so he and his wife moved to New Mexico. His first job was as a basketball coach at Lovington, New Mexico. In his second year, he won a state championship. Since they would not give Coach Tasker a key to the gym, he quit and moved to Hobbs, New Mexico.

3

BASEBALL

I didn't realize that Wahoo McDaniel was on the field since he wasn't eating raw hamburger meat. He was still mad at me for beating him at archery that summer in Boy Scout camp. Now I'm getting it from my coach and Wahoo.

My family is very competitive. Almost all were baseball players. I played summer baseball until I graduated from high school. My dad encouraged me to play. At best I was average since my heart was in basketball. My uncle, Chief Nicholson, played college baseball and football. He also played semi-pro baseball. His son, Chuck, played third base for Oklahoma State and was drafted by the St. Louis Cardinals but declined and went on to have a great career in the air force. After going to summer camp, Chuck saw that the Cardinals had the best third basemen in baseball and made me to play baseball, but it wasn't in my heart.

Chief told me a funny story and it was hard for me to believe. I told it to my dad, and he laughed and said that it was true. As the story goes, Blackwell, Oklahoma was forming a sand lot baseball team. Dad, his two brothers, Chief and his brother Bobbie, plus the Ackerson brothers, formed a Blackwell sandlot team. They were young and rearing to go. They had their first game in Ponca City, Oklahoma and Ponca City was good. When they took the field, they suddenly realized that they only had eight players. They were trying to figure out how to place two players in the outfield instead of three. An old man walked over and offered to be their ninth man. He was obviously a farmer.

"Have you ever played baseball?"

He answered, "A little."

"Do you have a glove?"

"No, I'll just play barehanded!"

"Okay, get in right field."

To make a long story short, the old farmer was at bat four times. The Ponca City pitcher felt sorry for the old man and threw a nice soft pitch. The old man hit the ball and slowly made it to first base. Everyone laughed watching the old man. The fourth time at bat was serious—the winning run was on second base. The pitcher threw his best pitch for strike one. The farmer stepped back and rubbed his eyes. Time out was called to see if he was alright. Then the old farmer stepped back into the batter's box. The pitcher threw his best pitch. A loud sound of the bat hitting the ball and it resulted in an unbelievable homerun.

Later as the team was celebrating the win and drinking beer, one of the Ackerson brothers ask the old farmer, "You said that you played a little baseball, but where?"

The old man took another drink and answered, "The Chicago Cubs."

4

FULL COURT PRESS

One of coach Tasker's philosophies is the rotation of players. Tasker believes you have to rotate at least eight players, but more is better. The rotating players were all starters. The advantages gained from rotating players include:

1. Fouls were spread over eight or more players, so there's a better chance of having key players at the end of the game when you need the best.

2. You are more likely to run down your opponent.

3. Practice goes better if the players know they will play an important part of the game.

To me, it seemed as if Coach Tasker was rotating players like the Pony Express! Just as there are advantages to rotating players, there are also drawbacks. Just like in little league baseball, if the umpire calls a strike on their son, parents will attack the umpire. If the parents see the coach removing their son from the game, they will dislike the coach.

Coach Tasker started each practice with a one-on-one full-court drill. At the end of practice, the coach would end with the black line drill. At this time, I didn't realize that Coach Tasker, aka "Tip," was a genius with a unique personality. During the summer, a load of us coaches drove out to Albuquerque for the all-state game and coaching clinic. While sitting with Tip during a practice session, some coach came up and asked Coach Tasker about his full-court press.

Basically, it's a defensive strategy where the defending team applies intense pressure on the offensive team across the entire length of the court, from one baseline to the other, to disrupt their offensive plays, force turnovers, and prevent easy scoring opportunities. There is pressure from the start. The defending team applies pressure on the ball handler right from the moment they inbound the ball, rather than waiting for them to get into a half-court setting. There's man-to-man defense where each defender is responsible for an individual player, or a zone defense, where players cover designated areas of the court. The objective of a full-court press is to force mistakes, such as turnovers, steals, or rushed decisions, while also wearing down the offensive players physically and mentally.

Within a minute, Coach Tasker had the man believing he was the best coach in the state with a perfect full-court press. Tip was a great motivator of men. Since we used the full court press, it was rare for our opponent to apply a full court press against us. Still, we had a press offense that we worked on every practice. I like it when my team would shift into the press offense without calling a timeout.

5

COACH TASKER AKA TIP

Every Sunday after church at 2 pm, Coach Tasker opened the gym for three-on-three games. Then, after about two hours of fun on the hardwoods, I would drink a Pepsi Cola with Tip. One Sunday, he had a bright idea. Why teach an offense? Any time you have to spend more than five minutes teaching an offense, it's not very good. When we play three-on-three, all we do is free-lance. You know, pass and cut or screen and roll or screen away and keep the offense spread and the floor balanced.

Come practice on Monday, it took Coach Tasker less than five minutes to implement his idea. That was in the early 1960s. Now, everyone is running this free-lance style of offense. People think that this of-fense was started at the college level by Bobby Knight or Dean Smith, but that is wrong. It was developed by a high school coach.

I was just starting my first year of college when I became friends with Bill Bridges. Bill was a sophomore in high school. Even as a high school tenth grader, Bill was big at 6'5"and 200 pounds. During the summer, we would play one-on-one. When Bill and I played, I would beat him every time. As a junior, I would win two out of three games. When Bill was a senior, I would win about half the time. After Bill spent one year at Kansas University, I couldn't seem to get a shot off. Bill improved in his defense, and his quickness gave him a huge advantage.

When Bill was a sophomore at Kansas University (KU), he invited me to come to KU for the NCAA Regional Tournament. Bill introduced me to Wilt Chamberlain. He was the tallest person that I have ever seen. My eyes almost popped out. He looked like a creature from another planet; the top of my head hit him about belt buckle high. Another time in the pros, Wilt was slam dunking when Bill, who was playing on the other team, blocked his shot. The following summer Bill confided in me that Wilt could have torn his arm off, but he let up for a friend.

Wilt went on to play for the Harlem Globetrotters before joining the National Basketball Association (NBA), where he played for the Philadelphia / San Francisco Warriors, Philadelphia 76ers, and Los Angeles Lakers. Standing 7 ft 1 in tall, he played center for fourteen seasons. In 1978, Wilt was enshrined in the Naismith Memorial Basketball Hall of Fame and elected to the NBA's 35th, 50th, and 75th anniversary teams.

The summer program that Coach Tasker ran was amazing. During this summer, a program for grade school and high school emerged. Coach would spend the day as a referee. So, one night, he asked Bill Bridges and me to ref the last night's league game. We were honored to help.

During the game, I called a foul on a big guy—a 6'7"black man. The big guy came over to me and told me that if I called another foul on him, he would tear my head off. He was serious. Bill heard him and said something like, "If you want to beat someone up, then start with me. After you tear my head off, then you can go after Frazier."

The big guy slumped down and didn't say a word. Bill later fouled him out of the game and then to the bench. I saw him slip out the back door before the game was over. The incident reminded me of a game between Kansas University and Missouri. A fight broke out. There was a picture in the Kansas City newspaper of Bill Bridges with the entire Kansas coaching staff standing behind him.

The great Coach John Wooten of UCLA said that his team used the full-court press for the entire game. He said in every game, there was a two-minute explosion, where UCLA would outscore their opponent by twenty or more points.

Coach Tasker held the record of the National Coach of the Year award and a national title for Hobbs's 160-plus points against Carlsbad's 120-plus points; now that's an explosion in a thirty-two-minute game!

Coach Tasker told me that the new superintendent called him into her office and said, "It's time that we give a younger man a chance at coaching. You may finish this season, but next year we want a younger man coaching our boys' basketball."

"Thank you for allowing me to finish this year," Tip responded.

And so, the great coach who won nineteen state championships was fired. This was a man who was devoted to his teams and basketball.

The superintendent then said, "Turn your keys in at the end of the basketball season."

Coach Tasker worked his last two years as an assistant coach to the girls' team. The head girls' coach was one of Tip's former players. Tip died at 79 or 80 years of age. The gym is named Tasker Field House in his honor.

6

ELK CITY & THE BIG ELKS

After four years under Coach Tasker, I got my first high school basketball coaching job in Elk City, Oklahoma. The Pony Express system of play worked, and we won more than was expected.

As a basketball coach, I was completely devoted to developing a winning program. But I had enemies that I was entirely unaware of. The athletic director and head football coach told me there could be no basketball as long as football was going on. The state allowed basketball to start around October 1st, but not in Elk City!

"You may start your program the week after football," I was told.

"Yes, sir," I answered.

However, I knew a gym off the school grounds, located at a church. I was also an assistant football coach. So, after my duties were over, I opened the gym at the church. Of course, the head football coach who was also the athletic director found out that we were shooting baskets.

"I saw you in the gym shooting baskets with Gary Woody," Coach J said.

"Yes, sir," I answered.

"I want you to understand that this is a football school. We have basketball but here basketball is a minor sport. There is to be no basketball until football is completely over."

"Yes, sir, but you had your last game Friday, and basketball is going on all over Oklahoma," I answered.

"If I see you in the gym while football is going on again, I will fire you. By the way, I picked you to be our basketball coach. We had five high school coaches who were more qualified than you. You were coaching junior high in Hobbs, New Mexico. I picked you because you were the least qualified."

"Sir, I just want to do my best in my first high school coaching job."

"Okay, but don't you ever start your program while football is going on again," Coach J said.

I got up from my chair, shaking in my shoes. He told me he would fire me and that I would never coach again. This really scared me, so I tried to please him. On a side note, I worked with our non-footballers on free throws. One evening, I hit one hundred free throws in a row, to everyone's amazement.

Finally, football season was over, and one of my starting players, Ron Rainey, a football player, reported to practice with a knocked-down shoulder. He was right-handed, and thank goodness it was his left shoulder that had the issue. However, it was hard for him to shoot or rebound.

Our season started, and our team was getting better at the press and fast break. I was still in trouble for my extra work with the team. This must be the only occupation that you can get in trouble for hard work. Our first season was good—better than expected—but not great. We won nineteen games and lost nine while Hobbs, New Mexico, was winning another State Championship.

I had an ally in the editor of the Elk City newspaper, a man named Larry Wade. After watching our team play, the newspaper of Elk City would always call our team the Big Elks. This went on for years. Now they were calling us the Go, Go, Elks!

In my second year, we were in the finals of the district tournament. The game was tied, and we had the ball in the backcourt. Just then, a time-out was called.

I gave the team strict instructions. "I want Gary Woody to take the shot! If Gary is covered, then Sammy Despain can shoot the last shot, but under no circumstances will Ted Jobe take the game-winning shot."

I had a towel in my hand. Our inside man was covered, and the last second was about to clear. Oh, no! Sammy's covered, and Ted Jobe shot at the last second. I covered my head with my towel. I heard the crowd roar! I peeked from under the towel, and they were carrying Ted on their shoulders. I looked at the score clock. We had won by two points!

The next week, we won the regional tournament, which qualified us for the state tournament in Oklahoma City. We won our first game and advanced to the semi-finals against Comanche. They couldn't handle our press, and with fifty seconds to go, I decided to put some of our sophomores in the game. Our twenty-point lead suddenly turned to a fourteen-point lead, and I had to get those sophomores out of the game. We won by twelve points.

After the game, one of the parents, Mr. O'Hara, came to me and said something that would be a once-in-a-career statement, "Coach, you will be playing for the State Championship. Don't put my son, Ronnie, in the game."

I responded, "Mr. O'Hara, you got it."

In the state finals, we were up against the co-player of the year, a 6'6" black player who was averaging close to thirty points per game. His coach had him bring the ball down against our press. He did a great job but only scored about half his normal points.

With twelve seconds left in the game, their coach called for a time out and we had the ball. Something happened that I have never heard of before or since. Our 5'7" Sammy Despain ran over and got in their huddle. He listened to their coach, then ran back to me and announced, "Coach, they are going to press us!"

We were delighted; we worked every day on the press. It was like throwing Brer Rabbit in the briar patch. They had no one guarding the inbound passer, so we gave the ball to Sammy, and he took it down the court and passed it to our all-stater, Gary Woody, who drove down the lane and scored the winning basket. As they carried me off the floor, I saw two of my high school teammates from Blackwell, Oklahoma. I smiled and waved!

We were returning to Elk City after our team won the first boys' State Championship in the history of the school. On Monday, I proudly carried the State Championship trophy to school. That school year of 1966-1967, I was awarded the Coach of the Year in Western Oklahoma!

***

Earlier in the year before I was fired, the principal told me that the superintendent wanted to talk to me. So, as the principal watched my science class, I walked to the superintendent's office.

"We want you to coach the golf team this spring," the superintendent said.

I looked at him, thinking I had some exposure to golf in high school. I knew that I didn't like golf and was not good at the sport. I responded, "No, sir, I don't play golf. I don't like golf, and I'm sure not going to coach it."

"No? You want to work here again next year?"

I said, "OK, I'll coach golf." That was the best decision I could have made. I didn't know it, but this was good for me. I'm now eighty-eight years old, and I'm still playing golf.

When I was in high school, I had a superhero; it was Superman. While I liked Batman, Superman was better because he could fly. And on the same level as Superman was Arnold Short. Arnold was a three-time all-American basketball player from Oklahoma City University. He had a fall-away jump shot that was deadly accurate and almost impossible to block.

Arnold Short was in Elk City, and he came right up to me at a quarterbacks' meeting and asked me to play golf. I was happy to say, "Yes!" to his request.

That evening, we teed the ball up at the Elk City Golf and Country Club. I noticed that Arnold had an expensive set of golf clubs, and my clubs were so cheap that I was embarrassed. On the first hole, there was a tree to the left of the fairway. I usually hit my drive to the tree. I made it to the tree, and Arnold drove his ball twenty yards past the tree. I was on the first green in regulation with a 30-ft putt for birdie. Arnold had a 3-ft putt for birdie. He got a birdie while I had a bogey. Not talking about the rest of the round, but I was rubbing shoulders with one of my idols. That was a great day for me, and I was really happy that Elk City made me do the golf thing!

Back in Elk City, there were some shenanigans afoot. My dad had a cousin who was a member of the Elk City School Board. He told me that while he was absent during a board meeting, the board had voted to fire me. I later found out that the athletic director/head football coach had me fired, but after we won the State Championship, they had an emergency meeting and reversed their decision. I had never been fired before, and it hurt deep down.

The following summer, I paid a visit to my old friend, Coach Tasker. While in his living room, he received a phone call from one of his former players at Lake Charles. They needed a basketball coach at one of their high schools.

Coach Tasker said, "I have a coach right here in my living room who I will recommend. He just won state in Oklahoma."

The next thing I knew, I was on a plane to Lake Charles, Louisiana.

7

LAKE CHARLES – HEAD BASKETBALL COACH

It was 1968 when I flew down to Lake Charles for the job interview; it was my first time in the state of Louisiana. I loved everything about Louisiana at first glance—the people, the food, the trees, and the water.

My family and I were looking at the amazing bridge as we drove into the city. The bridge was so tall that it disappeared into the clouds. I thought it looked like the gates to heaven. On the other side, we could see the lakes. Lake Charles had a real meaning.

The job paid about four thousand dollars more than Elk City. I gave away my home in Elk City and accepted their offer. My new wife and I were on our way to Lake Charles. We bought a home near McNeese College and settled into our new life in Louisiana. I loved my new job at the high school. The La Grange Senior High School was made up of three grades, including sophomores, juniors, and seniors. I really liked the principal and the coaches whom I would be working with. As I met the boys I would be coaching, I told them they were part of a great program. La Grange had won the State Championship back in 1967 with a great coach and a great player. When La Grange had those same conditions, it would happen again.

The first year was really good. We were the Gators, and we won a big tournament in Lake Charles. Then we won our district and went on to win two games in the state playoffs. Our second year was very similar. In Louisiana, they have the Top Twenty, which consists of the top four teams in each class going on to play in Alexandria, Louisiana. The city is located in the center of the state, so all schools come together there, making the trip easier for those teams who have made it into the Top Twenty. My third year was the best. We won thirty games and made it to the Top Twenty Tournament. Things were good, but under all the excitement, our enemy was raising his head. I was totally unaware and believed all was well. The fourth year at La Grange was like my third until my top rebounder suffered an injury. That injury caused us to lose a key game in our district. We made the state playoffs but not the Top Twenty. Still, our fourth season was a good year.

During the summer, the school gave all the coaches summer jobs. Everyone did driver's education, except me. I was on duty in the library. In my second year, I tried to do a "Coach Tasker" by running a summer basketball program. Coach Tasker of Hobbs, NM was paid money and had assistant coaches to help. I didn't get paid nor did I have help. I also refereed the games. I was pleased to see my basketball players develop, but it was hard work. During the third summer, the program had become popular and some of the football players formed a team. I had watchful guardian angels taking care of me.

I believe in guardian angels, and those angels were working overtime. It made me think of a time when I was in the ninth grade. One of my friends was shooting his new 30 ought 6 rifles. He shot at a thick steel, and the bullet ricocheted, striking me in the head. The doctor gave me a shot and sewed up the wound. He jokingly said, "It went in until it hit cement. Your dad was in last week, and he told me about your first goal and the five-gallon bucket. And you can't go swimming with that head. Stay out of the pool all summer."

Louisiana also had something that I had not experienced. Fishing. Growing up in West Texas, you don't learn the ins and outs of fishing. Hunting, yes; fishing, no. So, when one of my coaching friends invited me to go fishing, I quickly said, "Yes!" I went to the nearest sporting goods store and bought a fishing rod and reel, along with a mini bucket. We were going to the Big Burns Reserve to fish. It was beautiful!

In a boat on the lake, we were drifting across a large expanse of water. My friend was at the front of the boat casting lures. He was bringing in a beautiful bass. I did my bit, too. Every time I cast my line with the cork, sinker, and a hook with a wiggle shiner. In seconds, I got hung up.

"Wayne!" I yelled, "Let's throw an anchor and stop drifting."

"No!" he responded. "Out here, we fish with lures!"

As we drifted, I was getting hung up on various branches and weeds in the lake. Then I noticed a shallow spot, about waist-deep, so I told Wayne to let me out.

"OK, just let me out. I'll fish here. You can come back and pick me up in a few minutes," I said. Right away, the cork sank below the surface, and I had a two-pound bass. While putting the bass on the stringer, I saw something that scared me. A twelve-foot alligator was swimming toward me. I immediately yelled to Wayne, "I want back in the boat! Now!"

Unfortunately, sound travels over the water, and I could hear Wayne laughing. The alligator swam within ten feet of me and then crawled up on an embankment. In the meantime, Wayne pulled up. I was not happy as I climbed back into the boat.

"Damn it, he could have killed me and had me for dinner!" I angrily responded.

"He's just sunning himself," Wayne said with a smile on his face. "If he had wanted you, you would have never seen him coming!"

I looked at Wayne with a frown and said, "Shut up and give me one of those lures."

Like all referees, I had my run-in with certain referees. The association would send the coaches a list of referees we were allowed to blackball; we could reject two from the list.

My favorite ref was an elderly bald man named Mr. B. He would run over to our huddles and plead with me to slow down the pace of the game. Mr. B was having problems keeping up with the game. This would encourage my team to speed up and keep the pressure on.

During one game against our toughest opponent, the coach from the other team was in tears. "Please slow it down!" This shut up the crowd and I felt sorry for him. He didn't know how to teach his team to run an offense against a full-court press. We had the full-court press taught to me by Coach Tasker. So, I called off the press, and by halftime, they were starting to catch up to us.

Our principal came to our locker room and said, "Put that press back on them!" Like I needed help to determine when to turn the pressure back on.

The second half was a runaway. I was really feeling sorry for them. As we were walking down the hallway my team and I heard and saw their coach kick his file cabinet up against a wall and then throw a book over his desktop. I felt sorry for him but in time I would get fired despite my success. All the football coaches at my school would watch my end.

I laugh when I think about being the head coach and being held back by my assistant when I was going after a referee. I got mad at the referee when he called a foul on my team and then said something ugly to me while showing off to the crowd.

My bald-headed referee friend came to my school to talk to me about how much of a problem it was for him to referee our games. I told him in other areas they have three referees on the floor to cover the game. He said, "We might need four in your games."

I have coached in four different states and in my humble opinion, I thought Oklahoma was best. Kansas was second, New Mexico third, and Louisiana last. Sorry, Mr. B!!

***

When I was a senior in high school at Blackwell, OK we were having a career day. Some of us wanted to be coaches and met with a Junior College basketball coach. The only thing I can remember him saying is, "Listen to me. Do not go into coaching! You will be sorry."

Years later I could see his wisdom. You can be very successful, work as hard as anyone can, and in the end, still get fired!

About this time in history, our government passed a law called "Freedom of Choice." So many schools closed the black school, and all the students attended the same school. This caused some conflict between the school and parents.

When I started my first year in Lake Charles, I liked the fact that all the coaches had a free hour. I decided to jog for two miles and work out on the weights. Jogging came easy but lifting weights took more discipline. I was doing the bench press at 150 pounds. All the football coaches were lifting over 200 pounds. I enjoyed the camaraderie of the other coaches. I didn't know that I was in trouble of being fired. This was a fun group, and I still had my shooting eye for basketball. I thought that I had made the right choice to follow my love for the five-gallon bucket. Then I could remember a favorite teacher of mine back in Andrews, TX. He called me into his office and showed me my drawings in Industrial Arts. He had put them on his bulletin board.

"You have a good eye for art," he said. "You could go to Texas Tech like I did and get a major in Architectural Engineering. You would make lots of money and never worry about being fired."

I wonder if I made a mistake. When I was in my mid-seventies I was still a big-time jogger. Then one day I got a bad case of plantar fasciitis. That ended my two-mile jog. I still did some weightlifting. By my mid-eighties, the only thing I did was play golf. I would start and my feet would hurt. My knees would wobble and be very weak. My hands had the shakes and one of my eyes had macular degeneration. And I was facing a ten-foot putt.

***

Are you familiar with Nancy Lopez? I had a great encounter with this former professional golfer when she was a young girl. Like Arnold, Nancy Lopez was one of golfing's greats. She became a member of the LPGA Tour in 1977 and won forty-eight LPGA Tour events, including three major championships.

While visiting my mom and dad in Roswell, New Mexico, my dad wanted to play golf. I didn't have my clubs with me, so we played out of his golf bag. When we were on a par 3 hole, I noticed this old man and his little girl playing behind us. They had their hands on their hips, acting like we were playing too slowly. I waved them on. As it turned out, the old man wasn't playing, but the little girl teed her ball up. I smiled and turned back to putt my ball.

The girl's shot almost hit me, and the ball rolled up to the cup about ten feet away. It was one hundred and fifty yards, and she put her ball up there like the pro she would become.

When we got back to the clubhouse, I told the pro, who just laughed and said, "Oh, that was Nancy Lopez and her dad. She is twelve years old, and she won the women's amateur golf tournament this year in New Mexico." I couldn't believe it!

***

When June and July passed, I wanted to visit my parents in New Mexico. But the football coach called me into his office. He was being nice.

"Man, you have really worked hard this summer," Coach C, the athletic director and head football coach, said. "Come here and look at my calendar." He pointed at his wall calendar. "We start football here." He pointed to an August date. "This is when we start football. I hear you are going to visit your parents in New Mexico. Since you worked so hard, why don't you take another week and show up on this date?"

"Thanks, Coach, see you in August!" I said with enthusiasm.

"See you then," Coach C said with a grin.

The next thing I knew, I was in the principal's office getting fired for being a week late to August football practice. It was a setup, but I was too dumb to see it. Thinking back, I believe Coach C was jealous of our successes. What other occupation can you work as hard as you can and become a success, only to get fired? I was stupid enough to believe him. I had to uproot my wife and kids to find another job.

My best lesson was to separate my so-called friends from my true friends. True friends will not stab you in the back.

8

JONESBORO HODGE – HEAD COACH

I applied for the basketball coaching job at Jonesboro Hodge High School. At that time in Louisiana, there were high schools that were all black or all white students. There were two small towns that consolidated into one school called Jonesboro Hodge High School. I met with their superintendent.

"I like your school and would like to be the biology teacher and head basketball coach, but I refuse to be an assistant football coach," I said to the superintendent.

"Why?" he asked.

"I'm just saying, if you want your basketball coach to work as an assistant football coach, then I am not your coach," I said.

"Okay, okay! I get it. You will not help our football program. But we will have some black players. We have a new law called Freedom of Choice. We closed our black schools and everyone will be going to our high school," he said.

The Freedom of Choice policy was controversial. The Supreme Court declared racial segregation in public schools was unconstitutional. Some states and school districts resisted school desegregation.

"That is not a problem with me," I said. "I will give everyone a fair chance. But no football!"

I got the job and in addition to being the basketball coach, I was a science teacher. See, my guardian angel was watching over me!

Jonesboro Hodge High School had lots of talent and pretty good facilities. I wanted to do my best here. My first two years were great. State playoffs and thirty wins per year. During my third year, an incident occurred with the football team. They had won their first four games when the local country club wanted to give a party to celebrate the victories. The football team was invited, but they made it clear that none of the Black players were invited.

The Black players took things into their own hands and crashed the party. The end result was the school board threw all the Black players off the team, and they were not allowed to participate in sports for the rest of the year. This caused the football team to lose most of their games. They then gave the football coach the principal's job at the elementary school, and I lost one of my best players. Still, we won almost thirty games. We lost in a double overtime to DeRidder, LA, to go to the Top Twenty.

My fourth year was moving along, and though it was clear that we had lost some of our better players, we were winning more than we lost. The high school principal called me into his office and dropped a blow on me. He said, "We want you to cut all of the Black players off the team, except for the ones who are starters. You don't need a bench full of Black players."

I just stared at him for a moment and then said, "Sir, that would destroy our basketball program. We're talking about ninth and tenth graders. They play on our junior varsity. I will not cut those young players."

"Do you know that you can be fired for refusing an order from a superior?"

"I had a nightmare the other night. I dreamt that you made me cut all the Black players, and they had nothing to keep them busy, so they formed a gang and went around stealing and destroying property. It was an awful nightmare. I'm sorry, but I can't do that," I said.

The principal slammed a book on his desk and gave me a "go to hell" look.

I got up and left his office. This was outright racism, and I was swimming in it. "I sure hope they don't find out that I'm a registered Cheyenne Native American from Oklahoma," I thought. Plus, my mother would throw me out of the family if she thought I would judge people by the color of their skin.

We had trouble in the next games. I had two white boys who started and were good players. But they were acting strangely, which caused us to lose the game. It made me mad since I thought they were deliberately throwing the game.

Later, when I got on the bus, I could smell something. Someone was smoking! I got really mad, and yes, I used some cuss words. It was very quiet going home. The next day, the superintendent called me to his office. "Heard you were using profanity on the bus," he said.

"Yes, I really got mad. Sorry, I won't do it again," I answered.

"Well, I want you to resign. We can't have our coaches cussing out the players," the superintendent sputtered.

"Yes, sir, you got it," I responded.

From the coaching perspective, I really liked Jonesboro Hodge. But I found out later that the police caught a man selling illegal drugs at one of the popular businesses. My white basketball players were regular customers. If I had known that I would have thrown that at the superintendent!

I really loved Louisiana, but I wanted to go back north where racism was not so bad, and drugs were not as popular.

9

COFFEYVILLE, KANSAS

I was thrilled to get hired as the basketball coach and biology teacher at Coffeyville, Kansas. The old basketball coach, who I was replacing, was made assistant principal. We both had graduated from Pittsburg State University in Pittsburg, Kansas. We both had played college basketball for the great John Lance.

They told me that the basketball program was down. "Just give it your best." The first half of the season was not too good, then the Pony Express system caught on, and we ended the year by qualifying for the state tournament. We were rated eighth, so we had to play the number one seed. With one minute to go, we had a one-point lead. I could see that everyone was concerned, even the referees. We lost by one point at the buzzer. The game was on the Kansas State University floor. I could see that everyone was happy with the turnaround.

The following year in our district, we were close to the top but lost to Pittsburg, Kansas, to go to the state. Our district, from top to bottom, was even. Every game was close, but no state tournament. Our third year was much like the second, a good year, but we didn't make it to the state tournament. During our fourth year, I started getting criticism from the team's parents. One mother called me complaining that her son didn't know if he qualified for a letter jacket and that I didn't explain the standard for getting a letter jacket. One man met me on the basketball court and said his son was cut from the "B" team. I didn't know that our B-team coach had cut his son. I did agree with my "B" team coach. I was just happy that the dad did not beat me up.

We made it to the state in my fourth year at Coffeyville. We were seeded eighth again, and we played the number one seed, which was a Wichita high school. At Wichita State University, we missed a short shot at the buzzer that would have won the game. The following Monday, I was summoned to the principal's office.

"The parents don't like you, and I'm sorry to tell you this, but you are fired," the principal said.

I went to see a lawyer, who said, "Your record is good. You being fired is not in line with the record." Then, he went on to say, "With your hair cut like that, you look Native American."

I responded, "I'm a registered Cheyenne."

"Can you prove that?" he asked.

I took my Indian card out and showed him. The lawyer took a deep breath and said, "Give me a dollar and I will represent you in a court of law. I think I can get you a big chunk of money. However, you will never coach again."

"No, no, I don't want to sue anyone," I answered. Then I got up and walked out.

I moved back to Oklahoma City and in one year earned a second master's degree in guidance counseling. While sitting at the dinner table one evening, the phone rang.

"This is the athletic director in Gonzales, Louisiana. I was talking with the high school principal from Lake

Charles. He gave you a big recommendation. He said you were the hardest working coach they ever had, and your teams were Top Twenty-bound. Would you consider coaching our basketball team here?"

"Okay, but where is Gonzales?" I asked.

"We're located on I-10 between Baton Rouge and New Orleans."

So, I went to Gonzales, the Jambalaya Capital of the World!

10

GONZALES, LOUISIANA

After my conversation with the athletic director and head coach, he made it look good, and I had no other objections. So, I accepted the job. One thing that caught my interest in Gonzales was that it was located near the Atchafalaya Swamp. I bought a boat and was looking forward to some fishing. The swamp was full of alligators, snakes, and all kinds of fish. My son, Ricky, was old enough to join me in fishing.

What I was not told was Gonzales had just built a new high school. So, the student population was split, and the new school was getting most of the basketball players. Gonzales would be playing in a tough Baton Rouge league.

Gonzales was the Jambalaya Capital of the world. I got a rented house, and my daughter, Lynn, and my son, Ricky, moved in. Next, the A.D. head football coach introduced me to a lawyer who had a son in junior high. The season started with some big wins, and I could see some potential in our players. We were having a winning year. Our school played in a tough Baton Rouge district. Halfway through basketball season, I got the news from the A.D. who hired me that the lawyer didn't like me and, "Oh yeah, you're fired."

"Hells bells, why? How have I offended him?" I asked.

"It's your style of play. His son came to a game. He doesn't think he can play due to his lack of speed. You're in love with that fast game, full-court press, and fast break... hell, a person would have to be a big-time athlete to play for you! If you would slow it down, play a game, and walk the ball up the court—"

"Okay, fire me. I'm not going to change my game to please the lawyer."

That conversation put me into a deep depression. Why can't people see that you can't be a winner in basketball and walk? You have to run. Thank goodness there was a member of the school board who stood up for me, and I got one more year with Gonzales. Then I thought of my first basket—the five-gallon bucket. That was the start of all this misery... that five-gallon bucket!

At the end of my second year, I was looking for another home. My son, Ricky, and I had enjoyed fishing in the Atchafalaya. We learned never to make more than one turn on the swamp, or we would be lost and eaten by mosquitoes!

I got a call from a football coach from Texas. He offered me a job over the phone. He had talked to someone at a coaching clinic. I thanked him, but I didn't want to go to Texas. I was thinking of retirement, and I would be starting over in Texas. Finally, I heard from a small country school near Lake Charles. I called the principal, and I was hired.

I don't know why, but I thought God was real. I was bouncing back from one setback after another. My deep belief in God and his guardian angels gave me hope. The summer between my ninth grade and tenth grade year, I became a true follower of my Lord and Savior Jesus Christ. I was about fifteen and on my way to the scout ranch in the Davis Mountains.

Surviving the incident of getting shot in the head and then the summer at the Boy Scouts ranch in the Davis Mountains made me believe. Yes, my parents dragged me to church every Sunday, but this was a real-life experience.

I was selected by my troop to be initiated into the Order of the Arrow, an honor society within the Boy Scouts of America (BSA). It recognizes Scouts and Scouters who exemplify the Scout Oath and Law in their lives and promotes brotherhood, cheerfulness, and service. It is designed to provide a program of leadership development and community service while fostering a deeper understanding of Scouting traditions and values. With the initiation, the entire group of Boy Scouts must first be assembled. The members of the Order of the Arrow were present and dressed in Native American regalia. I felt a surge of excitement as a ball of fire flew down from the mountain and lit the campfire. Very impressive, but I later found out that it was a container full of kerosene set on fire that ran down a wire to the fire pit. Each boy who was going through the initiation from every troop was called out. First, they put a reef around our necks, and it had thorns. We were given two matches and told if we could start a fire then we could burn the thorny reef.

We were then blindfolded and led by two members of the Order of the Arrow into the mountains. We were warned that during an earlier initiation, a scout went to a different valley, and it took them three days to find him. He had lost weight and had an encounter with a mountain lion. They promised that we would be led to our campsite within two miles of the Boy Scout ranch and must find our way back by 8 a.m. the next day.

On my way to my campsite, I fell into a stream. I could tell that they were taking me upstream. I thought I was so smart. All I had to do was go down-stream, and I would be back to the camp, ready to start the rest of my initiation, which was to work all day.

Finally, they reached my campsite. "You have to start your fire, and then you can burn the reef," one of them said.

I removed my blindfold and started gathering wood. This is going to be easy, I thought. We were allowed a flashlight, two matches, and a blanket. I reached into my pocket to get my two matches. They were wet, and I thought I was so smart when the stream current hit my legs. I could not get my fire to light. So that meant the reef would be on my neck all the next day. I snuggled up in my blanket and I couldn't get the thought of mountain lions out of my mind.

About 2 a.m. I gave up on sleeping and started walking back to camp. I tripped and broke my flashlight. Now I was in the dark, and I thought that I heard the cry of a mountain lion. I needed to hurry back to camp. Then I tripped again and fell into the stream. The only good thing was that the thorny reef floated down the stream. Suddenly, another night scream filled the air, and I fell on my knees.

"Dear Lord, please send help. Thank you, God, for your angels. Please send a guardian angel! I don't want to get lost, and it will take them three days to find me."

I got up and started walking along the stream. After about an hour, I could see a big change. The trees were larger, and the water was flowing faster. I must be going in the wrong direction. I stopped and turned around, and said out loud, "God, help!" Then I saw movement from the trees and an animal walked towards me. I stood shaking in my shoes. I looked toward the noise, expecting to see a mountain lion or at least a bear. Instead, a dumb-looking donkey walked right up to me.

I didn't know what to do, so I reached out and grabbed the donkey's tail. After about an hour of following this donkey, I saw another scout. He gave me the don't talk sign since another part of our initiation was to go 24 hours without talking. I followed him, and we both met the 8 a.m. deadline. We worked until supper time, and we were promised three square meals. They gave us a cracker and a square piece of cheese. The day ended at midnight with a big meal and a hardy congratulations.

The last day was Sunday, and the scoutmaster invited a preacher to give a sermon. I had promised God that I would be faithful, but at the end of the sermon, the preacher asked us all to close our eyes and bow our heads. Then he said, "If any of you had a religious moment during the week, please raise your hand." Then he said, "No one can see you. Raise your hand!" I peeked, and no one that I could see raised their hand. I was so ashamed that I didn't have the strength to

proudly raise my hand. Now I know how the disciples
and the twelve apostles must have felt, especially when
Jesus was crucified.

11

LONGVILLE, LOUISIANA - HEAD BASKETBALL COACH

The thing that stands out about Longville was winning on the road. We won two games away, close to Lake Charles. On one occasion, a gang got on our bus while we were eating and stole our bag of basketballs. I ran down one of the gang members. He didn't have our basketballs, but he did turn on me with a knife in his hand. As the police siren sounded, I told the Black man that if he didn't want to spend the rest of his life in prison, he'd better run. He turned and ran, and I was relieved. Life has its scary moments, again and again. There were guardian angels all around me that night. If that guy had really wanted to hurt me, I wouldn't be here telling my tale today!

We made it to the finals of the tournament. One of our players, Mike, scored over thirty points, but we still lost the game at the buzzer. Longville was a small country school. My new Louisiana wife and I lived in a motor home across from the school. I pulled a "Ralph Tasker" by starting a summer basketball program. We had some players who showed promise. We were surprised by the early success that our basketball team was showing.

My Louisiana wife loved fishing, and we lived close to a great lake called Toledo Bend. This lake ran all the way from the dam in DeRidder, Louisiana to Shreveport, Louisiana. We bought a tent, and on weekends that were free, we went camping and fishing at Toledo Bend. We also enjoyed dives into the lake, where we could see about eighteen feet underwater. During the Longville stay, my two kids and I got licensed for scuba diving. I was reminded of when I was back in college at Pittsburg State. As a P.E. major, I was taking a swimming class. Our teacher (the swim coach) was on the phone. We were laughing and splashing, just making lots of noise.

The coach came in shouting, "Well, I'm glad no one drowned!"

The student sitting beside me was one of our football players, and he came back with, "Frazier, here, can out-swim your fastest swimmer."

Well, that created a situation that, despite my saying, "No, no, no!" they dragged me to the starting box to swim a fifty-meter freestyle race. I won by half a length. What they didn't know was that I was raised in West Texas, with no air conditioning. We would go swimming every day just to stay cool. I was also in the Boy Scouts, and I only lost one swim race when I was disqualified for jumping the gun. The swim coach spent the next week trying to recruit me.

"I'm on the basketball team, on a scholarship. Our swim team doesn't have scholarships."

"OK, but you have a swim coach who was telling you that you have more potential as a swimmer than a basketball player," he responded.

Basketball-wise, we were okay at Longville, but I missed the state playoffs and the Top Twenty tournament. However, I was thankful that I was not fired.

During my second year at Longville, our basketball team started getting stronger. We were winning almost every game, but I wasn't too popular with some of the parents. I was not fired in Longville, and we had two good winning seasons. Then, a job opened with a good program in Many, Louisiana, which was just up the road. This school was known for its basketball program. I called Many's principal, and he invited me up for an interview.

12

MANY, LOUISIANA

The town of Many was north of Longville but was still on Toledo Bend. Many had lots of basketball talent and good facilities. The school principal took me over to a lawyer's office. They interviewed me. Yes, I thought that was strange, but he hired me.

During that summer, I drove three times a week to Many to open the gym. I did this at my own expense throughout the summer so I could meet the players, and they could play three-on-three and shoot baskets. When I walked into the gym, all the black players sat on one side of the bleachers while all the white players congregated on the other side. They did not like each other, and their parents hated the other group. I somehow had to coach this team. It made me sick wondering how I was going to do this.

Running the road brought back an old memory from my last year at Pittsburg State. It was in the spring, and school was almost over. I was lying in the student lounge watching TV, when in walks the richest fat boy on campus. He saw all of us lying around and loudly proclaimed that basketball players were in better shape than football players.

It was the year when our football team won the national NAIA Football Championship. The fat boy with a pocket full of money said, "I will bet $100 that Jack can beat all of you on a two-mile run." In about twenty minutes, the $100 was covered.

We went over to the track—a two-mile run was eight times around the track. I beat the football players by running the two-mile run in under eleven minutes. The fat boy collected his winnings and didn't give me a dime. "If you wanted money, then you should have put your money in the pot." That started all kinds of races. One basketball player ran home, which was about eighty miles.

Before school started, I found a house. We moved and got our kids in school. My Louisiana wife was delighted as we were right next to Toledo Bend Lake.

When the season started, I made sure that the lawyer's son started, and he was a pretty good player. Then came the Pony Express system. I had good players, and we won almost all of our games. By Christmas, we had only lost one game, and I thought everyone was happy. Then just before Christmas the principal called me into his office.

"I hate to tell you this, but you are fired."

"Why?" I asked.

"Well, the lawyer doesn't like your style of play," said the principal.

My heart fell to my stomach. Time and time again I had been mistreated as a coach. "Can he do that?" I asked.

Then he said something that I'll never forget. "Coaches are like bus drivers. If you don't like the way they drive, then get another driver."

I had never heard that before, so I asked, "Can I at least drive the bus to the end of the year?"

"I think that will be okay," he answered.

By Christmas break, we had only lost one game, yet the lawyer had the principal fire me. The lesson I learned (you young coaches listen and pay attention) was that the person you meet first is the one who will fire you.

13

Buras, Louisiana - Head Basketball Coach

My last stop in Louisiana was Buras, located on the Mississippi River. My Louisiana wife, Mary, and I drove to Buras at their invitation. They were looking for a basketball coach and a biology teacher. They took us out for lunch and looked over my credentials. We had a nice visit, and then they offered me the job. Buras had teachers' apartments, so we moved in during the summer. The town was located on the Mississippi River, just up from the mouth of the river! We discovered that the redfish ran up the river, and we would fish around the old fort.

We were catching some beautiful redfish, and we didn't know that the fishing was only good at certain times. So, we were giving fish away! When school started, I enjoyed the students and the other teachers. I didn't have to coach football. So, in October, I started basketball.

I was surprised to see that I had some good players. Our first season was good. We were playing in and around New Orleans. Things were looking good, then in my fourth year, "shit" happened. A new private school was built; they hired a Black coach who had played NFL football. Right after this, all of our best black athletes, most of whom were ninth and tenth graders, transferred to the private school. We were left with no basketball players in our junior or senior classes. While the team showed improvement, we lost every game.

We started with three sophomores and two freshmen in the strong New Orleans District. But then I remembered something that Coach Tasker had once said.

I had asked Coach Tasker, "What are the key components of a great basketball program?"

His answer was simple but true. "Ninety-three percent of any great program are the players. Then maybe seven percent is the coach."

It was a disastrous year. We did not win a game! If we came close, it was like a victory. When the season was over, the principal called me into his office.

"We decided to hire a black coach. We think that some of our black players will return. Sorry, Frazier, but we are firing you as a basketball coach. However, we want you to stay as our biology teacher and golf coach," the principal said.

I couldn't believe what I was hearing. I suddenly felt deeply depressed. I couldn't even speak. As I was going out to my car, I thought, well, I almost qualify for a Louisiana retirement. I'll stay, get my retirement, then move back to Oklahoma.

So they hired a black coach. Guess what? Not one of the black players returned and the coach resigned halfway through the season. Eventually, the old principal retired, and his assistant was moved up. He came to me one day as I was taking out the trash and wanted to know if I would mind coaching the basketball team. I didn't answer; I first gave him my best "go to hell" look. He got the message.

We had a week off and I decided to go to Grand Isle for some scuba diving and fishing. We put in our boat, which was a bit small for going offshore. Spotting an oil rig, we headed out to it and tied up to it. I think it was eighty to a hundred feet deep in that area. With my scuba gear on, I slid into the water while hanging onto the side of the boat. Mary spotted a shark that was longer than the boat we were in.

She said, "I think that is a tiger shark!"

As it swam by, my son, Ricky, looked down at me and said, "Don't hyperventilate, Dad! It's just a shark!"

I guess the shark didn't want to eat me and swam away. We all took turns scuba diving and fishing the rest of the day. Thank God we had guardian angels watching over us on that trip.

Altogether, I spent ten years in Buras, and I qualified for a Louisiana retirement. I took my retirement and moved back to Oklahoma City. What I learned from my life is that there is a God in heaven, and He has guardian angels.

My Louisiana wife received some tragic news that her ex-husband, the father of her children, was killed in a car wreck. As a result, she and her children were given a huge sum of money. So, she and her kids left me and moved to Baton Rouge, Louisiana. Our marriage was over, and she moved into a beautiful home near the Louisiana State University campus.

14

OKLAHOMA CITY

After returning to Oklahoma City with a Louisiana retirement, a little better than fifteen hundred dollars a month, I applied for a job teaching biology at U. S. Grant High School. I got the job, and when they read my resume, they asked me to work with the girls' basketball program as an assistant coach. I still felt a deep depression from Louisiana, but I could see that the girls' basketball coach needed help, so I agreed.

Towards the end of the season, they had a faculty basketball game against the boys' junior varsity. The game was played in front of the entire student body. I was asked to play, and I said no. I was fifty-five years old at the time and told them not to count on me. The girls pestered me to play and I gave in. I played for nearly three quarters and again saw the five gallon bucket. The faculty won, and one of the varsity players, who refereed the game, ran over all excited and said, "Coach Frazier, you scored twenty-eight points!"

"No way," I responded. "Maybe fourteen points."

"No, you hit five three-pointers, five for five at the free throw line, and four drives. That's twenty-eight points!"

"Oh my gosh!" I had completely forgotten about the three-point baskets. I suddenly became a hero to the girls' basketball team and some of my biology students. My depression ended and I felt great again!

Then I remembered what Coach Tasker told me when I drove to Hobbs for their Christmas tournament. He said, "If you were playing today with the three-point basket, you would be highly recruited!"

Later, the assistant principal called me into his office. He started by complimenting my shooting. Then he told me that the girls' basketball coach had resigned and asked if I would be interested in taking the position.

He got a quick "No!" from me! The five gallon bucket had got me into enough trouble. In my younger days, so many of my so-called friends were jealous of the little success I enjoyed. Without a second thought, I declined the offer! "I'm done with coaching."

The following summer, a guidance counseling job opened at the Canadian Valley Technical Center. I applied and got an interview. One question that came up during the interview was, "Sir, do you play golf?" This question came from the head guy.

"Why, yes, I do," I responded.

The head guy got up and, as he was walking out the door, said, "If he has the proper credentials, hire him."

It made me so happy since I had taken that one year to get a master's degree in guidance counseling.

"Does your boss play golf?" I asked.

"Oh, yes, and since you also golf, you are hired!"

Oh my gosh! I'm so lucky that Elk City made me coach the golf team! I have played golf off and on for over twenty years. Still, I'm not a good golfer. Wait a minute, I have never had a private golf lesson! I quietly set up a lesson in Oklahoma City.

"Okay, Jack, hit some shots. Let me see where you are, then we'll go from there," my instructor said.

What he said next blew my mind. "Well, Jack, you have a good body, but you lack the skill."

I could have punched him in the nose! But by the end of the lesson, I was hitting the ball to the left with a slight draw. Sitting in my car about to go home I remembered, by an act of God, I once shot a hole in one which was the pinnacle of my golf career. My closest moment to greatness in golf occurred when I took Ricky to the New Orleans Open. I wanted Ricky to see the pro golfers play.

Between the ninth and tenth holes is a bathroom. I was standing in line when a hand touched my left shoulder. Then a voice said, "Fellows, may I play through?"

I looked and it was Jack "the Golden Bear" Nicklaus, one of the greatest golfers of all time. We let him pass ahead and he did his business and then rushed over to the tenth hole to continue his round. I still have the shirt that the Golden Bear touched.

I started at Canadian Valley Technical Center and immediately felt the difference between being hired as a coach and being hired as a guidance counselor. As a guidance counselor, I was treated as a professional.

I have a college degree and two master's degrees. My job was to travel to all the surrounding schools to visit eighth, ninth, and tenth graders. I would describe all the programs of CVTC to the students and list the advantages of taking one of these programs. A lot of the student thought if they went to the technical school, they couldn't go to college so I had to show them how they can use our programs as a springboard to continue their education in college. One student took our auto mechanics program and then earned a college degree in mechanical engineering. I was back to being happy Jack Frazier. I liked the professional courtesy. People were kind. I loved it.

My first session as a guidance counselor was at Mustang High School to speak to ninth graders. Their teacher introduced me to the class and said, "If you give this man any trouble then you will be in big trouble. I'm going to the teachers' lounge." She turned and walked out of the room. She whispered to me, "Are you afraid to be by yourself?"

Lady, I have faced an alligator in the swamp in Louisiana, a tiger shark in the Gulf of Mexico, and a twelve-inch knife in Lake Charles. I started my presentation and suddenly thirty students laid their heads down and started to fall asleep. One student started to snore.

"Can anyone in the classroom tell me who is the president of the United States?" I asked. No response from the classroom. "Okay, I have this chocolate candy bar here for the student who can tell me who is our president?" A tiny girl in the front row gave the correct answer. "That is correct," and I reached into my bag and pulled out a candy bar to give it to her. I started to see heads rise and then asked, "What is the name of the school I represent?" A boy answered with the correct name of my school, and I pitched him a candy bar. Now everyone was awake and ready. The teacher returned to her classroom to see all her students listening and in their seats. I made a mental note to always have candy bars everywhere I go.

The only other incident was when I was asked to take a group of our students to the gym. We had one show-off who hit five free throws in a row. He didn't know me or anything about me. He and the whole class knew that I was a Ropes instructor. We had a ropes course set up along the Canadian River.

We would take our students one class at a time to the Ropes course. But now the little show-off was wanting to embarrass me in front of the whole class. I hit thirty-five in a row and another teacher asked me, "What is that all about?"

"Once upon a time there was the five-gallon bucket," I responded.

She looked at me with a blank stare like she didn't know me and said, "Oh."

Things at CVTC were going great for about five years. Then orders came from the state level to eliminate the recruiting counselor position! My boss gave me the bad news. The surrounding schools started calling my boss and telling him that the greatest thing that CVTC had going was Jack Frazier! The greatest compliment of my life! Oh, how those candy bars were paying off.

Finally, my boss came to my office and said, "Okay, we found some extra money. If you are in agreement to just work three days a week, you can stay."

I agreed, but I worked five days for lower pay. After a year, my pay went back to normal. I worked another eight years at CVTC and qualified for Oklahoma retirement.

Then the second greatest compliment came my way. The boss came to my office and said, "I hear you are wanting to retire. Is that true?"

"It's true. I'm sixty-eight and I'm tired. I want to play golf," I said.

"Could you give us one more year?" he asked.

"I'm sorry but I've made other plans," I said with some regret. And with that, I finished my work at Canadian Valley Technology Center.

I retired from Oklahoma at the age of sixty-eight and now live full-time in New Mexico. Being a guidance counselor was a whole new experience. I was treated with respect, and everyone was nice. It blew my mind, and when I retired, the boss came to my office and tried to get me to stay at least one more year. I loved it!

15

FINAL THOUGHTS

I hope my story sends a message to stop treating coaches like bus drivers. In my opinion, it should be against the law to fire a coach unless he has committed a crime. I have even heard of coaches who were fired at half time during a game. Coaches want to see their athletes succeed. Most coaches played the sport with some success. Even so, too many coaches have been fired, and it was not their coaching but pure politics.

Schools often have parents who have great influence on the academic and sports departments. Maybe they have made a donation or are on the school board. My message is, "Pease stop firing coaches!" Coaches have spent their entire lives in one or more sports. They want your sons and daughters to be winners in life. Once a coach has been fired at any level, they should not be treated like a doormat. If a coach does not report for duty on time or throws a chair across the court, fine them! If a football coach snaps and runs on the field to tackle a ball carry, don't fire him (or her)! They need help. Fine him and get him some professional help.

If a lawyer, who is also a parent, comes into the main office and wants the coach fired, tell him that he doesn't run the school. Don't fire the coach. If the coach has not committed a crime but used profanity, fine him, but don't ask him to resign. Coaches are the hardest-working people on the faculty. They are not bus drivers who can be dismissed for no good reason. Most coaches learn the sport from the ground up—from that five-gallon bucket. Not to mention that most coaches have families. Their wives and kids are hurt because their dad or mom is treated like a bus driver.

To the administrator in the state of Louisiana who told me that coaches are no more than bus drivers and who said, "If you don't like the way they are driving, then get another bus driver," here's what I have to say: "This is so wrong! Coaches are more like police officers. The only way you can fire a police officer is if they commit a crime. The same should be true for coaches."

Coaches want their players to be wise and succeed in life. Coaches at all levels are being fired all across this country. There is no other profession where a man or woman can work for longer hours, be so dedicated to the job, and then be fired. In the professional sports leagues, coaches are fired during half-time! It should be against the law to fire a coach who has not broken the law! Even if the coach has lost every game, they don't deserve to be fired. Don't fire this professional who is trying his best to turn things around.

***

Before ending this book, I'd like to add a note about addiction. Spending my life as a high school teacher, counselor, and coach, I have noticed that most people have some sort of addiction. An addiction can be destructive, such as causing a person to steal to support their habit, causing a person to be overweight, and more. A person that can control bad addictions is a strong, smart person.

The jails and prisons are filled with people that have failed to overcome a bad addiction. I am 88 years old and still dream of basketball. I still love the sport. It has given me lots of fun and lots of misery. When I was four years old, we lived in the country. My dad, who was raised on a farm, had two milk cows. In the 1940s in West Texas, there were open pastures to graze animals. So, my dad bought a horse. At age four, I would ride this horse to bring in the milk cows. I loved that horse. When I turned seven, my family moved into town. Dad sold the horse, and I was the saddest kid in Texas.

Was I addicted to that horse? Was I addicted to basketball? I don't know; however, they both brought joy and misery. Addictions can cut someone's life short. Give it some thought...

***

Prior to WW2, the five-gallon bucket was shorter but wider. Today, this bucket is taller and slimmer. Over the years, I learned that the five-gallon bucket was much smaller than the regular-sized basketball goals. So, after spending hours shooting baskets as a kid, I discovered that the regular basketball goal was so big that I thought, "How can anyone miss that huge target?"

I have always lived from paycheck to paycheck. Now that I'm retired, it's from retirement check to retirement check, with an important Social Security check thrown in. With the passing of my parents, my sisters and I split their life savings. When I started receiving my Louisiana retirement, I thought that I could buy a Cadillac or invest in stocks. I chose stocks. I started buying BP Amoco stocks. My dad had worked for BP Amoco and invested in the company. One day, I decided to go to Edward Jones, a financial services firm, and hire a stockbroker or at least check to see what they offered. There I met Sang Tran, who has remained my financial advisor for many years and is a great broker.

My Oklahoma wife, Mary, and I are now retired in the Land of Enchantment. Thank God for New Mexico! We are enjoying the mountains, the wildlife, and the state's golf courses. Even more, we love the green chilis! (My Louisiana Mary is still fishing.)

"What the hell is that five-gallon bucket doing in our backyard?" My third wife from Oklahoma stood there with her hands on her hips. Mary was furious!

"Leave that five-gallon bucket alone! I'm working on my chip shots!" I answered.

16

PHOTOS

Jack sitting on Shorty (1940) with sister Judy

Jack Frazier

Frazier stings the Jackets for 2 points.

Jack Frazier

Jack Frazier

Coach Jack Frazier

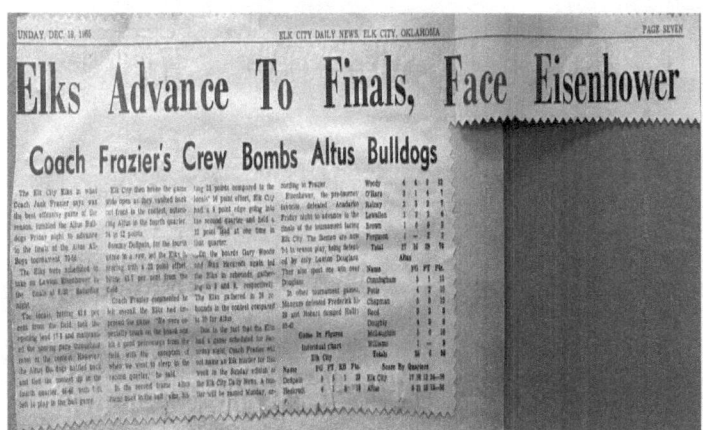

Elk City Daily News

Ralph Tasker and Jack Frazier, Hobbs, NM 1993

Ralph Tasker Arena

ELK CITY ELKS — Flanking Coach Jack Frazier on the left are (front to back, Ted Jobe, Tommy O'Hara, Ronald Rainey, John Thomas, Johnny Lewallen, Stan Heckrodt and Randy Ferguson. On the right are (front to back) Sammy DeSpain, Alphanso Wilcots, Pat Brown, Dwayne Rainey, Gary Woody and Larry Thompson.

Elk City Basketball Team

*Jack, Mary Webster, and Skeeter (2015) on the 10th
green, Angel Fire, NM*

Jack with his wife, Mary

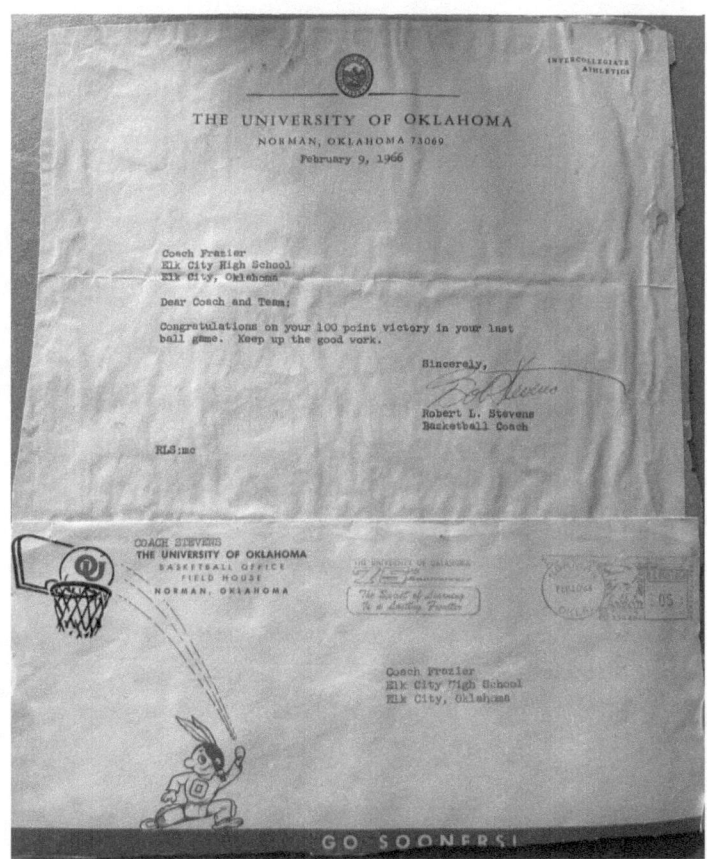

A Letter from OU Basketball Coach

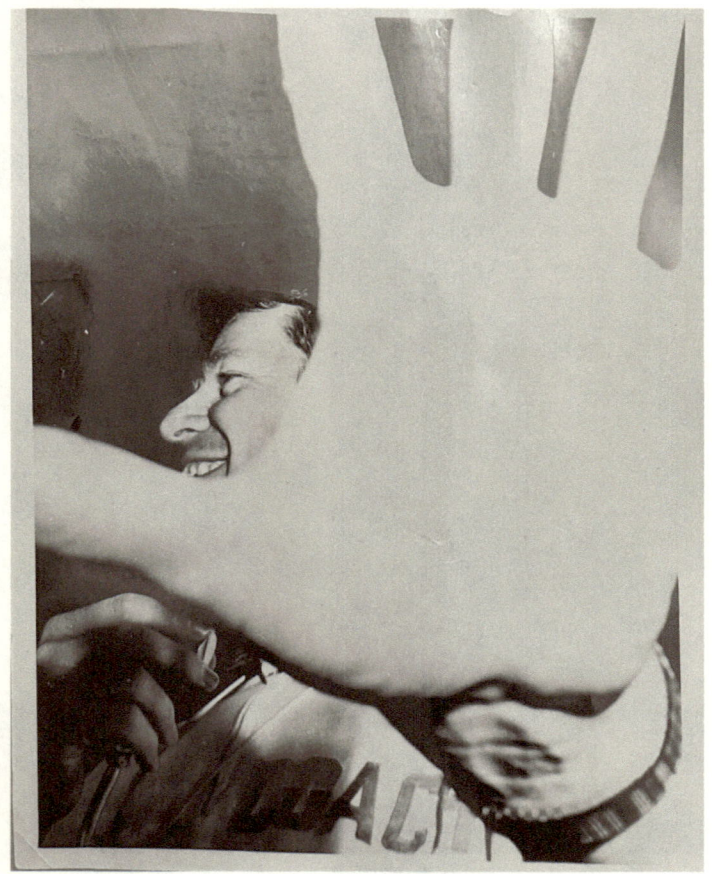

Jack Frazier awarded Coach of the Year

Jack Frazier

Jack Frazier takes home State Championship trophy

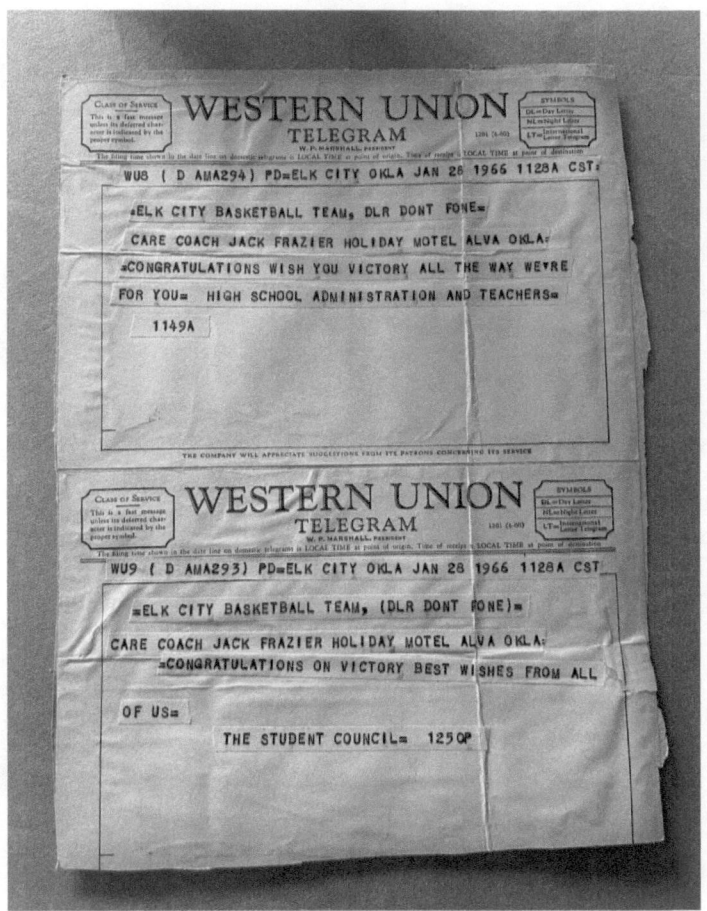

Western Union telegrams

Feb 27, 1966

AND HE RAISES THE SCORE— Gary Woody, 30, jumps out of reach
Joe Tucker, 31, and Bruce Williams, left, of Anadarko to dump in a basket
for Elks. Stan Heckrodt, 55, helps screen for three time winner of the
Hustler award, who bagged 9 points for Elk City. Anadarko won the
game, 61-60. (Staff Photo by Bob Wright)

Elk City vs Anadarko

El Reno and Elk City Scrimmage

Jack Frazier in Oklahoma

Randy Ferguson jumps and scores a bucket for the Go-Go Big Elks

December 19, 1965

Sammy DeSpain pops in two points for Elk City.

Elk City Basketball

Jack and Rick (son)

ABOUT THE AUTHOR

Jack Frazier loves basketball, but he wasn't always good at it. When he was in fourth grade, he made his first attempt at a free throw and failed. For his birthday, he asked for a basketball. When he went outside to shoot, he realized he didn't have a basket. Out in the garage was an old rusty five-gallon bucket—back then they were made of metal, short and wide. With a chisel and hammer, Jack quickly cut out the bottom, creating a basket, and the rest is history. Basketball was in his bones and in his dreams. He played in college at Pittsburg State University. At 5'11 3/4" tall, Jack was told he had the skills but not the height to play pro. He pursued coaching instead and became a high school basketball coach. In his short story, Five Gallon Bucket, Jack shares his experiences and thoughts on the sport, particularly from the lens of a basketball coach. His musings give basketball lovers a glimpse into this retired coach's story of how the five-gallon bucket gave him purpose. Jack is retired and lives in New Mexico with his wife. They split their time between Angel Fire and Alamogordo. When he's not dreaming about basketball, you can find Jack on the golf course.

www.ingramcontent.com/pod-product-compliance
Lightning Source LLC
Chambersburg PA
CBHW031435120626
46545CB00006B/2415